Camilla Urso

Choruses to be Sung at the Grand Musical Festival

Tendered by Camilla Urso in aid of the Mercantile Library of San Francisco

to be held on the afternoons of Tuesday, Wednesday, and Thursday,

February 22d, 23d and 24th, 1870

Camilla Urso

Choruses to be Sung at the Grand Musical Festival
Tendered by Camilla Urso in aid of the Mercantile Library of San Francisco to be held on the afternoons of Tuesday, Wednesday, and Thursday, February 22d, 23d and 24th, 1870

ISBN/EAN: 9783337222192

Printed in Europe, USA, Canada, Australia, Japan

Cover: Foto ©Thomas Meinert / pixelio.de

More available books at **www.hansebooks.com**

CHORUSES

TO BE SUNG AT THE

GRAND MUSICAL FESTIVAL

TENDERED BY

CAMILLA URSO

IN AID OF THE

Mercantile Library

OF SAN FRANCISCO.

TO BE HELD ON THE AFTERNOONS OF

TUESDAY, WEDNESDAY, and THURSDAY,

FEBRUARY 22d, 23d and 24th, 1870.

Programme.

☞ The Choruses mentioned below are alone to be sung at the approaching Festival.

APPENDIX.

Bacon & Company, Printers.

SACRED FESTIVAL-OVERTURE ON LUTHER'S CHORAL.

"A Strong Castle is our Lord."

NICOLAI.

GLORY TO GOD.

CHORUS. Allegro.
Luke ii. v. 14.
Soprano.
Alto, or 2nd Treble).
Tenore.
Basso.
Allegro.
♩ = 80.
f Glo-ry to God, Glo-ry to God in the high - - - est,
f Glo-ry to God, Glo-ry to God in the high - - - est,
f Glo-ry to God, Glo-ry to God in the high - - - est,
p and peace on earth,
f Glo-ry to God, Glo-ry to God,
f Glo-ry to God, Glo-ry to God,
f Glo-ry to God, Glo-ry to God,
Glo-ry to God in the high - - - est,
Glo-ry to God in the high - - - est,
Glo-ry to God in the high - - - est,
p and peace on earth,

f good will towards men, towards men, good will.
f good will towards men, towards men, good will to-wards men, to - wards
f good will.. towards men, to - wards men, good will to-wards
f good will to-wards men, good will.. to-wards men,
8vi.
.... towards men,..... to - wards men. Glory to God, Glo - ry to God in the
men, good will....... towards men. Glory to God, Glo - ry to God in the
men, good will towards men. Glory to God, Glo - ry to God in the
good will...... towards men. Glory to God, Glo - ry to God in the
high - - - - est, p and peace on earth,
high - - - est, p and peace on earth,
high - - - - est, p and peace on earth,

f good will, good will, good will,

f good will to-wards men, to - - wards men, good will, good will, good will,

f good will.... to - wards men, towards men, good will, good will, good will,

f good will, good will. good will,

f

8 8 8

good will to - wards men,............ good will to - wards men.

good will towards men, good will........ to - wards men.

good will towards men........ good will to - wards men.

good will.... to - wards men,...... good will to - wards men.

mf

8

tr

p *pp*

AND GOD SAW EVERYTHING THAT HE HAD MADE.
RAPHAEL.
RECIT.
ACCOMP.
And God saw ev'-ry thing that He had made, and be-hold it was ve-ry
good; and the hea-ven-ly choir, in song di-vine, thus clo-sed the sixth day:
ACHIEVED IS THE GLORIOUS WORK
CHORUS. Vivace.
Soprano.
Alto.
Tenor.
Basso.
VIVACE
♩=86.
A-chiev - ed is the glo - rious work;
A-chiev - ed is the glo-rious work; The
A-chiev - ed is the glo-rious work;
A-chiev - ed is the glo-rious work; The

The Lord be - holds it, and is
Lord be-holds it, and is pleas'd, the Lord is
The Lord...... be - holds it, and is
Lord be-holds it, and is pleas'd, The Lord be - holds it, and is
pleas'd, the Lord be - holds, and is well pleas'd.
pleas'd, the Lord be - holds, and is well pleas'd.
pleas'd, the Lord be holds, and is well pleas'd.
pleas'd, the Lord be - holds, and is well pleas'd. In lof - ty
In lof - ty strains let us....... re -
In lof-ty strains let us....... rejoice; let us re -
In lof-ty strains let us...... re-joice, In lof - ty strains let us re -
strains let us...... re - joice, let us re - joice, In lof-ty

-joice, In lof - - - - - - - - - - ty strains let us re - joice;
-joice, In lof - ty strains let us re - joice, let us re - joice; Our song let
-joice, let us re - joice; Our song let be............
strains, in lof - - - - - ty strains let us re - joice;
8va.
Our song let be the praise of God, Our song let
be the praise of God, the praise of God,
.... the praise of God, the praise of God, the praise of God, the praise of God,
Our song let be the praise of God
be the praise of God, the praise of God, the praise of God. In lof-ty strains
Our song let be the praise of God, the praise of God. In lof-ty strains
Our song let be the praise of God, the praise of God. In lof-ty strains

let us re-joice; Our song let be the praise of God, In lof-ty
let us re-joice: Our song let be the praise of God, In lof-ty
let us re-joice; Our song let be the praise of God, In lof-ty
strains let us re-joice; Our song let be the praise of God, the praise of God, the
strains let us re-joice; Our song let be the praise of God, the praise of God, the
strains let us re-joice; Our song let be the praise of God, the praise of God, the
praise of God.
praise of God.
praise of God.

No. 3. CHORUS.—"TO GOD ON HIGH."

No. 5. THE MARV'LOUS WORK.

SOLO and CHORUS. GABRIEL.

TREBLE VOICE.

Oboe Solo.

ALLEGRO.

♩=144.

p *fz* *f* *p*

The

mar - - v'lous, the marv'lous work be-hold a-maz'd, The glo - rious

p *f* *p*

hie-rar-chy of heav'n; And to th' ethereal vault resound,

f *p* *f*

The praise of God, The praise of God, and of the sec - ond day, and of the sec - ond

p *p* *mf*

SOLO.
day, And to th' e-thereal vault re - sound. The praise of God, The praise of
CHORUS.
SOPRANO. f
And to th' e-thereal vault re - sound, The praise of God, The praise of
ALTO. f
And to th' e-thereal vault re - sound, The praise of God, The praise of
TENORE. f
And to th' e-thereal vault re - sound, The praise of God, The praise cf
BASSO. f
And to th' e-thereal vault re - sound, The praise of God, The praise of
f
SOLO
God, and of the se - - cond day, and of the se - cond day. The
God, and of the se - - cond day, and of the se - cond day.
God, and of the se - cond day, the se - cond day.
God, and of the se - cond day, the se - cond day.
God, and of the se - cond day, the se - cond day.
p

marv'lous work be-hold a-maz'd, The glo-rious hier-ar - chy of heav'n ; And from th' e-the-real
(TREBLE.) CHORUS.
And
And
CHORUS.
And
And
f
vault .... re-sound the praise of God, and of the se - cond day.
from, and from th' e-the-real vault re-sound the praise of God, and of the se - cond day.
from, and from th' e-the-real vault re-sound the praise of God, and of the se - cond day.
from, and from th' e-the-real vault re-sound the praise of God, and of the se - cond day.
from, and from th' e-the-real vault re-sound the praise of God, and of the se - cond day.
Oboe.
p

SOLO.
The mar - - v'lous work behold amaz'd the glo - rious
hier - ar - chy of heav'n, And to th' e-the-real vault re-sound,
CHORUS.
And to th' e-the-real vault re - sound, And
And to th' e-the-real vault re - sound, And
CHORUS.
And to th' e-the-real vault re - sound, And
And to th' e-the-real vault, re - sound, And
f
p

the praise of God,
the praise of God,
to the vault re - sound,
the praise of God,
the praise of
to the vault re - sound,
the praise of God,
the praise of
to the vault re - sound,
the praise of God,
the praise of
to the vault re - sound,
the praise of God,
the praise of
p
f
p
f
and of the se - - cond day,
And to th' e-the-real vault ....
God, and of the se - - cond day, and of the se - cond day.
And to the
God,
and of the se - cond day, the se - cond day.
And to the
God,
and of the se - cond day, the se - cond day.
And to the
God,
and of the se - cond day, the se · cond day.
And to the

re-sound the praise of God, and of the se - cond
vault, And to th'e-the-real vault re-sound the praise of God, and of the se - cond
vault, And to th'e-the-real vault re-sound the praise of God, and of the se - - cond
vault, And to th'e-the-real vault re-sound the praise of God, and of the se - cond
vault, And to th'e-the-real vault re-sound the praise of God, and of the se - - cond
day.
day.
day.
day.
day.

THE HEAVENS ARE TELLING.

GABRIEL.
p To-day that is com - ing, speaks it the day,
URIEL.
p To-day that is com - ing, speaks it the day,
RAPHAEL.
p To-day that is com - ing, speaks it the day,
p The night that is gone to fol - low-ing night, The night that is gone to
p The night that is gone to fol - low-ing night, The night that is gone to
p The night that is gone to fol - low-ing night, The night that is gone to
Tutti.
fol - low-ing night. The hea - vens are tell - ing the glo - ry of God, The wonder of his
Tutti.
The hea - vens are tell - ing the glo - ry of God, The
Tutti.
The hea - vens are tell - ing the glo - ry of God, The won - der, the
fol - low-ing night.
Tutti.
The hea - vens are tell - ing the glo - ry of God, The won - der, the wonder of his
fol - low-ing night.

work, the won-der of his work dis - plays the fir - ma - ment,
won-der of his work dis - plays, dis - plays the fir - ma - ment, The
won-der of his work dis - plays, dis - plays the fir - ma - ment, The
work, the won-der of his work dis - plays the fir - ma-ment,
fz
8va.
The wonder of his work dis - plays the fir - ma - ment.
won-der of his work dis - plays, dis - plays the fir - ma - ment.
won-der of his work dis - plays, dis - plays the fir - ma - ment.
The wonder of his work dis - plays the fir - ma-ment
fz
p
GABRIEL.
p In all the lands re - sounds the word, nev-er un-per-
URIEL.
p In all the lands re - sounds the word, nev-er un-per-
RAPHAEL.
p In all the lands re - sounds the.. word, nev-er un-per-
p
p

-ceiv-ed, ev-er under-stood, ev-er, ev-er, ev - er un-der-stood.
-ceiv-ed, ev-er under-stood, ev-er, ev-er, ev - er un-der-stood.
-ceiv-ed, ev-er under-stood, ev-er, ev-er, ev - er un-der-stood.
In all the lands re-sounds the word, nev-er un-per-
In all the lands resounds the word, nev-er un-per-
In all the lands resounds the word, nev-er un-per-
-ceiv-ed, ev-er understood, ever, ever, ev - er un-der-stood, ever, ever,
-ceiv-ed, ev-er understood, ever, ever, ev er un-der-stood, ever, ever,
-ceiv-ed, ev-er understood, ever, ever, ev - er un-der-stood, ever, ever,

A Tempo.
Più Allegro. ♩= 144. Tutti.
ev - er,.... ev - - er un - der - stood. f The hea - vens are tell - ing the
Tutti.
Tutti. f The hea - vens are tell - ing the
f The hea - vens are tell - ing the glo - ry of
ev - - er,.... ev - - er un - der - stood.
A Tempo.
Tutti.
f The hea - vens are tell - ing the glo - ry of
ev - - er,.... ev - - er un - der - stood.
Più Allegro.
Voices alone.
p A Tempo.
f
glo - ry of God; The wonder of his work, the won-der of his work dis -
glo - ry of God; The wonder of his work dis - plays, dis -
God; The won - der, the wonder of his work dis - plays, dis -
God; The won - der, the wonder of his work, the won-der of his work dis -
- plays the fir - ma - ment.
- plays the fir - ma - ment.
- plays the fir - ma - ment.
- plays the fir - ma - ment. The wonder of his
8va

The wonder of his work...
The
The wonder of his work dis-plays the fir-ma-ment, the fir-ma-ment,
work dis-plays the fir-ma-ment, dis-plays the fir-ma-ment,
.... dis-plays the fir-ma-ment, the fir-ma-ment,
wonder of his work dis-plays the fir-ma-ment,
The won-der
The won-der of his work dis-
The won-der of his work dis-plays, dis-
The won-der of his work dis-plays the fir-ma-ment, the fir-ma-ment,
of his work dis-plays the fir-ma-ment,
The wonder
-plays the fir-ma-ment, The won-der of his work dis-plays the fir-ma-ment, The
-plays the fir-ma-ment, The won-der of his work, the wonder of his work dis-

The won-der of his work,..... the won-der
of his work... displays the fir - - ma - ment, The won-der of his work, dis-
wonder of his work dis - plays the fir - ma-ment,, the fir - ma - ment, The won-der of his
- plays the fir - ma - ment, dis - - plays, dis - - plays the fir-ma-
of his work....... dis - plays,..... dis - plays..... the fir - ma - ment,
- plays the fir - ma - ment, The won-der of his work....
work dis - plays,...... dis - plays..... the fir-ma-ment, dis -
ment, The won-der of his work dis - plays the
The won-der of his work dis-plays the fir - ma - ment, The
.... dis - plays dis-plays the fir - ma-ment, The
- plays.... dis - plays the fir - ma-ment, the fir - ma - ment,
fir - ma - ment,.......... the fir - ma - ment, The
8va

wonder of his work, the wonder of his work dis-plays, dis-plays the
wonder of his work, the won-der of his work dis-plays, dis-plays the
The wonder of his work dis-plays the fir - ma-ment, the fir - ma-
wonder of his work, the wonder of his work dis-plays, dis-plays the
fz
fir - - mament, The hea - vens are tell - ing the glo - ry of God, The
fir - - ma-ment, The hea - vens are tell - ing the glo -
-ment, The hea - vens are tell - ing the glo - - - ry of God, The
fir - - ma-ment, The hea - vens are tell - ing the glo - ry of God, The
fz
wonder of his work dis - plays the fir-ma-ment, dis - plays the fir-ma-
- ry of God, The won-der of his work dis
wonder of his work dis - plays the fir-ma-ment, dis-plays the fir-ma
wonder of his work................ dis - plays,................ dis -
Pedals.

-ment, dis - plays.................. the fir - ma - ment, The won-der of his
-plays the fir - ma - ment, the fir - - ma - ment, The won-der of his
-ment, dis - plays.................. the fir - ma - ment, The
-plays.................................. the fir - ma - ment, The won-der of his
Pedals.
work, the won-der of his work dis - plays, dis - plays the
work, the won-der of his work dis - plays, dis - plays the
won-der of his work dis-plays the fir - - ma - ment, the fir - - ma -
work, the won-der of his work dis - plays, dis - plays the
fir - - mament, The hea - vens are tell - ing the glo - ry of God, The
fir - - ma - ment. The hea - vens are tell - - ing are
-ment. The hea - vens are tell - ing the glo - - - ry of God,.........
fir - - ma - ment. The hea - vens are tell - ing the glo - ry of God,......
fz
fz

wonder of his work dis - plays,............ dis - plays...... the firmament, dis-plays the fir - ma-ment, dis-plays the fir - ma - ment, dis - plays the fir - ma - ment.

tell - ing the glo - ry of God,............ The won - der of his work dis - plays the fir - ma - ment, dis-plays the fir - ma - ment, dis - plays the fir - ma - ment.

.... The won - - - - - - - der of........ his work........... dis - plays the fir - ma - ment, dis-plays the fir - ma - ment, dis - plays the fir - ma - ment.

.... The won - der of his work dis - plays the fir - ma - ment, dis - plays the fir - - - - - ma - ment, dis-plays the fir - ma - ment, dis - plays the fir - . ma - ment.

fz fz fz fz fz

Pedals.

MOSES.
Then away with anxious fear. With ho - ly de-pendence, fervent prayers to
Lungi un va' - no - ti - mor. De - vo - ti, e pro - ni, fer-vi - de pre-ci al
Andante mosso.
God,.. come, let us of-fer, His divine pow'r and love humbly a - dor - - - - ing.
Di - o, fi - gli pre - ghi amo. Dal ce - les - to fa - vor tut - to spe - ria - - - mo.
Prayer in Moses in Egypt.
Andantino.
MOSES.
Oh! Thou whose pow'r tre - men - dous, Up - holds the star - ry
Dal tuo stel - la - to so - glio, Si - gnor ti vol - gi a
sky,...... Thy grace pre-serv - ing send us, To Thee, O Lord, we
noi:......... pie - tà de fi - gli tuo - i! del po - pol tuo pie -

ESTHER.
Thy grace pre-serv - ing, send us— To Thee, O Lord, we
Pie - tà de fi - - gli tuo - i, del po - - pol tuo pie
AARON.
Thy grace pre-serv - ing, send us— To Thee, O Lord, we
Pie - tà de fi - - gli tuo - i, del po - - pol tuo pie -
CHORUS.
Thy grace preserv - ing, send us— To Thee, O Lord, we
cry.
- - tà.
Pie - tà, de fi - - gli tuo - i, del po - - pol tuo pie
cry, we.... cry.
- - tà, pie - - tà!
cry, we cry. From wilds of fear - ful er - ror, Where -
- tà, pie - - - tà! Se pron - ti al tuo po - te - re so -
cry, we.... cry.
- - tà, pie - - - tà!
- in we dark - ly stray,.... Op-press'd with doubt and ter - ror, For sav - ing aid we
- no e - le - men - ti, e sfe - - re tu a - mi - co scam - po ad - di - ta, all dubbio er - ran - te

ESTHER.
Op-press'd with doubt and ter - ror, For sav - ing aid we
Pie - to - - so Dio! ne ai - ta! noi non vi - viam, che in
AARON.
pray. Op-press'd with doubt and ter - ror, For sav - ing aid we
piè. Pie - to - - so Dio! ne ai - ta! noi non vi - viam, che in
CHORUS.
Op-press'd with doubt and ter - ror, For sav - ing aid we
Pie - to - - so Dio! ne ai - ta! noi non vi - viam, che in
pray, we.... pray.
Te! che in Te!
ESTHER.
Oh, God of mer - cy, hear us, Our
La de - stra tua cle - men - te, spen -
pray, we pray.
Te! che in Te!
pray, we.... pray.
Te! che in te!

ESTHER.
Thee. Thy heal - ing pi - ty spare us, And bring us home to
- men. Il nostro cor che pa - ve deh tu con - for - ta ap-
AARON.
Thy heal - ing pi - ty spare us, And bring us home to
Il no - stro cor chè pa - ve deh tu con-for - ta ap -
MOSES.
Thy heal - ing pi - ty spare us, And bring us home to
Il no - stro cor che pa - ve deh tu con-for - ta ap -
CHORUS.
Thy heal - ing pi - ty spare us, And bring us home to
Il no - stro cor che pa - ve deh tu con-for - ta ap -
Thee, to...... Thee. Oh
- pien, ap - - - pien! Dal
Thee, to Thee. Oh
- plen, ap - - - pien! Dal
Thee, to Thee. Oh
- pien, ap - - - pien. Dal
Thee, to.......... Thee. Oh
- plen, ap - - - - - - - - - pien! Dal

Thou, whose pow'r tre - men - dous, up - - holds the star - ry
tuo stel - la - - - to so - glio, Si - - - gnor ti vol - gi a
Thou, whose pow'r tre - men - dous, up - - holds the star - - ry
tuo stel - la - - - to so - glio, Si - - - gnor ti vol - - - gi a
Thou, whose pow'r tre - men - dous, up - - holds the star - - ry
tuo stel - la - - - to so - glio, Si - - - gnor ti vol - - gi a
Thou, whose pow'r tre - men - dous, up - - holds the star - ry
tuo stel - la - - - to so - glio, Si - - gnor ti vol - - gi a
sky,............. Thy grace pre-serv - - ing, send us, To
no - - - - il pie - tà de fi - - - gli tuo - i del
sky,............. Thy grace pre-serv - - ing, send us, To
no - - - - il pie - tà de fi - - - gli tuo - i del
sky,............. Thy grace pre - serv - - ing, send us, To
no - - - - il pie - tà de fi - - - gli tuo - i del
sky,............. Thy grace pre - serv - - ing, send us, To

Thee, O Lord, we.. cry, To Thee, O Lord, we
po - - - pol tuo pie - - tà. del po - pol tuo pie -
Thee, O Lord, we cry, we cry, we
po - - - pol tuo pie - tà, pie - - - - - - - tà, pie - - -
Thee, O Lord, we cry, we cry, we
po - - - pol tuo pie - tà, pie - - - - - - - tà, pie - - - - - -
Thee, O Lord, we cry, we
po - - - pol tuo pie - tà, pie - - - - - -
cry, To Thee, O Lord, we cry.
- - tà. del po - pol tuo pie - tà.
cry, we cry, we cry.
- - tà, pie - - - - - - tà, pie - - - - - - - tà.
cry, we cry, we cry.
- - tà, pie - - - - - - tà, pie - - - - - - - tà.
cry, we cry.
- - tà, pie - - - - - - - tà.

Allegro Moderato ma con fuoco.
SOPRANO
f Thanks be to God! He laveth the thirsty
ALTO
f Thanks be to God! He laveth the thirsty
TENOR
TUTTI.
f Thanks be to God! He laveth the thirsty
BASS
more! Thanks be to God, He laveth the thirsty land. Thanks be to God! He laveth the thirsty
♩=126 Allegro Moderato ma con fuoco.
land, the thirs - ty land. Thanks be to God! He la-veth the thirsty land.
land, the thirs - ty land. Thanks be to God! He la-veth the thirsty land.
land, the thirs - ty land. Thanks be to God! He la-veth the thirsty land.
land, the thirs - ty land. Thanks be to God! He la-veth the thirsty land. Thanks be to
Thanks be to God, thanks be to God! The waters gather, they
Thanks be to God, thanks be to God! The waters gather, they
Thanks be to God, thanks be to God! The waters gather, they
God, Thanks be to God, be to God! The waters gather, they

rush a-long! they are lift - ing their voi - ces! The
rush a-long! they are lift - ing their voi - ces!
rush a-long! they are lift - ing their voi - ces!
rush a-long! they are lift - ing their voi - ces!
sf sf sf sf sf
waters gather, they rush along! they rush along! the waters gather, they rush along, . . .
The waters gather, they rush along! they rush . . . . a - long! the
The waters gather, they rush along! the waters gather, they rush long, they rush along!
The waters gather, they rush along! the wa - - ters gather, they rush a -
sf sf
. . . . see, they rush along! Thanks be to God! The waters gather, they
waters gather, they rush along! the wa -ters ga-ther, they rush along, they rush along!
Thanks be to God! He la - veth the thirsty land! The
- long! the waters gather, they rush along! Thanks be to God! He

rush along! the waters ga-ther, they rush a - long! He la - veth the thirs-ty
Thanks be to God! He la - veth the land: Thanks be to
waters ga-ther, they rush along, they rush a - long: the wa-ters ga - ther, they
la-veth the thirsty land! Thanks...... to.... to God, be to
land! The wa - ters gather, they rush along! Thanks be to God..........
God, thanks be to God........ The wa-ters gather, they rush a -
rush along! thanks be to God! Thanks be to God, thanks to
God, thanks! The waters ga - ther, they rush along! Thanks be to
.... He la - veth the thirs - - ty land! f The stormy billows are high, their
- - long, He la-veth the thirs - ty land! f The stormy billows are high, their
God! He la-veth the thirs - ty land! f The stormy billows are high, their
God! He la-veth the thirs - ty land! f The stormy billows are high, their
sf

fu - ry is mighty; The stormy bil-lows are high, their fu - ry is migh - ty;
fu - ry is mighty; The stormy bil-lows are high, their fu - ry is migh - ty:
fu - ry is mighty; The stormy bil-lows are high, their fu - ry is migh - ty;
fu - ry is mighty; The stormy bil-lows are high, their fu - ry is migh - ty;
ff
migh - ty their fu - ry:
f But the Lord is a-
migh - ty their fu - ry:
f But the Lord........ is a-
migh - ty their fu - ry:
f But the Lord.................. is a-
migh - ty their fu - ry;
f But the Lord.................. is........ a
sf sf sf
bove them, and Al-migh - ty, Thanks be to God! He laveth the thirsty land! The
bove them, and Al - migh - ty, Thanks, thanks be to God! The
bove them, and Al-migh - ty, Thanks be to God! to God! The
bove them, and Al-migh-ty, Thanks be to God, He laveth the thirsty land! The

stormy billows are high, their fu - ry is mighty: f But the
stormy billows are high, their fu - ry is mighty: f But the Lord....
stormy billows are high, their fu - ry is mighty: f But the Lord.........
stormy billows are high, their fu - ry is mighty: f But the Lord............. is....
Lord is a - bove them, and Al-migh - - ty. But the Lord.......
.... is a - bove them, and Al - migh - - ty. But the Lord........ f But the
.... is a - bove them, and Al-migh - - ty. But the Lord........ f But the Lord....
.... a - bove them, and Al-migh - - ty. f But the Lord.............
But the Lord is a - bove them, and Almigh - ty. Thanks be to God! He
Lord......... is a - bove them, and Al-migh - - ty.
.... is a - bove them, and Al-migh - - ty. Thanks be to
.... is......... a - bove them, and Al-migh - - ty.

la- veth the thirsty land. Thanks be to God! He laves the thirs-ty land. Thanks
Thanks be to God! He la-veth the thirsty land, He la - veth the land.
God! He la-veth the thirsty land, He la - - veth, la-veth the land. Thanks be to
Thanks............ Thanks be to God! He laves the land.
.... be to God, thanks! He la-veth the thirs - ty land.
Thanks be to God! thanks! He la-veth the land, the thirs - ty
God, thanks be to God! He la-veth the land, He la-veth the
Thanks be to God, He la - veth, He la-veth the thirs - ty land.
Thanks be to God, to God, thanks be to God, to God,
land. Thanks be to God, thanks be to God, thanks to
land, Thanks be to God, thanks be to God,
Thanks.......... Thanks.......................................

thanks be to God, thanks! The waters gather, they rush along; The waters gather, they
God, thanks be to God! The waters gather, they rush along; The waters gather, they
thanks be to God, to God! The waters gather, they rush along; The waters gather, they
thanks be to God! The waters gather, they rush along; The waters gather, they
rush along, they rush along, they rush along!
ff Thanks be to
God! He la-veth the thirsty land: thanks be to God, He laveth the thirs - ty land!
God! He la-veth the thirsty land:...... thanks.... He laveth the thirs - ty land!
God! He la-veth the thirsty land: thanks be to God, He laveth the thirs - ty land!
God! He la-veth the thirsty land: thanks be to God, He laveth the thirs - ty land!

INFLAMMATUS

(TO THY HOLY CARE.)

AIR AND CHORUS.

vir - - - go sim de - fen - sus per - te
let me be pro - tect - ed, Vir - gin
vir - - - go sim de - fen - sus in di - e ju -
let me be pro - tect - ed, On judg - ment, On
cres.
di - - - - - - - - - - - - - - - - ci - i
judg - - - - - - - - - - - - - - - ment day.
ff
ff
ff CHORUS.
In di - e ju - di - ci - i in di - e ju - di - ci - i in di - e ju
On the dread-ful judg-ment day, On the dreadful judg-ment day, On the dread-ful
ff
In di - e ju - di - ci - i in di - e ju - di - ci - i in di - e ju -
On the dread-ful judg-ment day, On the dreadful judg-ment day, On the dread-ful
ff
In di - e ju - di - ci - i in di - e ju - di - ci - i in di - e ju -
On the dread-ful judg-ment day, On the dreadful judg-ment day, On the dread-ful
ff
In di - e ju - di - ci - i in di - e ju - di - ci - i in di - e ju -
On the dread-ful judg-ment day, On the dreadful judg-ment day, On the dread-ful
ff
TREMOLO.

di - ci - i in di - e ju di - - ci - i
judg - ment day, the judg-ment, the judg - ment day.
di - ci - i in di - e ju di - - ci - i
judg - ment day, the judg-ment, the judg - ment day.
di - ci - i in di - e ju di - - ci - i
judg - ment day, the judg-ment, the judg - ment day.
di - ci - i in di - e ju di - - ci - i
judg - ment day, the judg-ment, the judg - ment day.
pp
pp
SOLO. SOTTO VOCE.
Fac me cru - ce cus - to - di - - ri
Thro' the lov'd Re-deem-er's dy - - ing,
Fac me cru - ce cus - to -
Thro' the lov'd Re-deem - er's
Fac me cru - ce cus - to -
Thro' the lov'd Re-deem - er's
Fac me cru - ce cus - to
Thro' the lov'd Re-deem - er's
Fac me cru - ce cus - to -
Thro' the lov'd Re-deem - er's

mor - - te chris-ti prœ-mu-ni-ri mor-te chris-ti
Let me fond-ly still re-ly-ing, Let me fond-ly,
di-ri mor - - te chris-ti prœ-mu-ni-ri mor-te
dy-ing, Let me fond-ly still re-ly-ing, Let me
di-ri mor - - te chris-ti prœ-mu-ni-ri mor-te
dy-ing, Let me fond-ly still re-ly-ing, Let me
di-ri mor - - te chris-ti prœ-mu-ni-ri mor-te
dy-ing Let me fond-ly still re-ly-ing, Let me
di-ri mor - - te chris-ti prœ-mu-ni-ri mor-te
dy-ing, Let me fond-ly still re-ly-ing, Let me
tr tr tr tr
prœ-mu-ni-ri con-fo-ve-ri gra - - -
still re-ly-ing, For sweet grace and mer - - -
chris-ti prœ-mu-ni-ri con-fo-ve-ri gra-ti-
fond-ly, still re-ly-ing, For sweet grace and mer-cy
chris-ti prœ-mu-ni-ri con-fo-ve-ri gra-ti-
fond-ly, still re-ly-ing, For sweet grace and mer-cy
chris-ti prœ-mu-ni-ri con-fo-ve-ri gra-ti
fond-ly, still re-ly-ing, For sweet grace and mer-cy
chris-ti prœ-mu-ni-ri con-fo-ve-ri gra-ti-
fond-ly, still re-ly-ing, For sweet grace and mer-cy

ff
ti - a.
cy pray.
a con - fo - ve - ri gra - ti - a
pray. For sweet grace and mer - cy pray.
a con - fo - ve - ri gra - ti - a
pray. For sweet grace and mer - cy pray.
a con - fo - ve - ri gra - ti - a
pray. For sweet grace and mer - cy pray.
a con - fo - ve - ri gra - ti - a
pray. For sweet grace and mer - cy pray.
ff
SOTTO VOCE
In - flam - ma - tus in - flam-
To thy ho - - - ly, To thy
ma - tus et ac - cen - sus Per te
ho - - - ly care a - lect - - - ed, Vir - gin

vir - - go sim de - fen - sus per te
let me be pro - tect - ed, Vir - gin
vir - - go sim de - fen - sus in di - e ju -
let me be pro - tect - ed, On judg - ment, On
cres.
di - - - - - - - - - - - - - - ci - i
judg - - - - - - - - - - - - - ment day.
ff
ff
ff
In di - e ju - di - ci - i in di - e ju - di - ci - i in di - e ju
On the dread-ful judg-ment day, On the dreadful judg-ment day, On the dread-fu
ff
In di - e ju - di - ci - i in di - e ju - di - ci - i in di - e ju
On the dread-ful judg-ment day, On the dreadful judg-ment day, On the dread-fu
ff
In di - e ju - di - ci - i in di - e ju di - ci - i in di - e ju
On the dread-ful judg-ment day, On the dreadful judg-ment day, On the dread-fu
ff
In di - e ju - di - ci - i in di - e ju - di - ci - i in di - e ju
On the dread-ful judg-ment day, On the dreadful judg-ment day, On the dread-fu
ff

di - ci - i in di - e ju - di - - ci - i
judg - ment day, the judg-ment, the judg - ment day.
pp
p SOLO.
Fac me cru - - ce cus - to - di - ri
Thro' the lov'd Re - deem - er's dy - ing,
mor - - te chris-ti præ - mu - ni - - ri
Let me fond - ly still re - ly - - ing,
SOTTO VOCE.
Fac me cru - ce cus - to di - ri mor - te chris-ti præ-mu -
Thro' the lov'd Re-deem - er's dy - ing, Let me fond - ly still re -

mor-te chris-ti præ-mu-ni-ri con-fo-ve-ri
Let me fond-ly still re-ly-ing, For sweet grace and
ni-ri mor-te chris-ti præ-mu-ni-ri con-fo-
ly-ing, Let me fond-ly still re-ly-ing, For sweet
ni-ri mor-te chris-ti præ-mu-ni-ri con-fo-
ly-ing Let me fond-ly still re-ly-ing, For sweet
ni-ri mor-te chris-ti præ-mu-ni-ri con-fo-
ly-ing, Let me fond-ly still re-ly-ing, For sweet
ni-ri mor-te chris-ti præ-mu-ni-ri con-fo-
ly-ing, Let me fond-ly still re-ly-ing, For sweet
tr tr tr tr ff
gra - - - - - - - - - - - - - - - - - ti-
mer - - - - - - - - - - - - - - - - - cy.
ve-ri gra-ti-a con-fo-ve-ri gra-ti
grace and mer-cy pray. For sweet grace and mer-cy
ve ri gra-ti-a con-fo-ve-ri gra-ti
grace and mer-cy pray. For sweet grace and mer-cy
ve-ri gra-ti-a con-fo-ve-ri gra-ti-
grace and mer-cy pray, For sweet grace and mer cy
ve-ri gra-ti-a con-fo-ve-ri gra-ti-
grace and mer cy pray. For sweet grace and mer-cy
ff

a. con - fo
pray. For sweet
a. con - fo ve - ri
pray. For sweet grace and
a. con - fo ve - ri
pray. For sweet grace and
a. con - fo - ve - ri gra
pray. For sweet grace and mer
a. con - fo ve - ri gra
pray. For sweet grace and mer
ve - ri gra - ti - a
grace and mer - cy pray.
gra - ti - a
mer - cy pray.
gra - ti - a
mer - cy pray.
ri - ti - a con - fo - ve - ri
cy pray. For sweet grace and
ti - a con - fo - ve - ri
cy pray. For sweet grace and

con - fo - ve - ri gra - ti - a.
For sweet grace and mer - cy pray.
con-fo-ve-ri gra - ti - a.
For sweet grace and mer - cy pray.
con-fo-ve-ri gra - ti - a
For sweet grace and mer - cy pray.
gra - ti - a.
mer - cy pray.
gra - ti - a.
mer - cy pray.
fff

CHORUS.—"SEE, THE CONQU'RING HERO COMES."

JOSHUA.

* Generally sung as a Trio.

DUET, OR CHORUS OF WOMEN.

FULL CHORUS.
TREBLE
f See the conqu'ring he - ro comes, Sound … the trumpets, beat the drums;
ALTO
f See the conqu'ring he - ro comes, Sound the trumpets, beat the drums,
TENOR
f See the conqu'ring he - ro comes, Sound the trumpets, beat the drums;
BASS
f See the conqu'ring he - ro comes, Sound…. the trumpets, beat… the drums;
Sports…. pre-pare, the lau - rels bring, Songs…. of triumph to…… him sing.
Sports…. pre-pare, the lau - rels bring, Songs … of triumph to…… him sing.
Sports pre-pare, the lau - rels bring, Songs of triumph to…… him sing.
Sports pre-pare, the lau - rels bring, Songs of triumph to…… him sing.
See the conqu'ring he - ro comes, Sound…. the trumpets beat the drums.
See the conqu'ring he - ro comes, Sound the trumpets beat the drums.
See the conqu'ring he - ro comes, Sound the trumpets beat the drums.
See the conqu'ring he - ro comes, Sound…. the trumpets beat…. the drums.

54

HALLELUJAH!

for the Lord God om - ni - po - tent reign - eth. Hal-le - lu - jah! Hal-le-lu-jah! Hal-le -
for the Lord God om - ni - po - tent reign - eth, Hal-le - lu - jah! Hal-le-lu-jah! Hal-le -
for the Lord God om - ni - po - tent reign - eth. Hal-le - lu - jah! Hal-le-lu-jah! Hal-le -
Ped. 8vi.
- lu - jah! Hal-le - lu - jah! Hal-le -
- lu - jah! Hal-le - lu - jah! for the Lord God om - ni - po - tent reign - eth. Hal-le -
- lu - jah! Hal-le - lu - jah! for the Lord God om - ni - po - tent reign - eth. Hal-le -
8vi.
Ped
- lu-jah! Hal-le-lu-jah! Hal-le - lu-jah! Hal-le-lu-jah! for the Lord
- lu-jah! Hal-le-lu-jah! Hal-le - lu-jah! Hal-le-lu-jah!
- lu-jah! Hal-le-lu-jah! Hal-le - lu-jah! Hal-le-lu-jah! Hal-le-lu-jah! Hal-le -

God om-ni - - po-tent reign - - eth. Hal-le-lu-jah! Hal-le-lu-jah! Hal-le-lu -
Hal-le-lu-jah! Halle-lujah! Halle-lu-jah! Halle-lu-jah! Hal - le - lu -
- lu-jah! Hal-le-lu-jah! Hal - le - lu - jah! Hal-le-lu-jah! for the Lord
Hal-le-lu-jah! for the Lord
8 Ped. 8

jah! Hal-le-lu-jah! Hal - le - lu - jah! Hal-le-lu-jah! Hal-le-lu-jah! Hal-le-lu-jah!
- jah! Hal-le-lu-jah! Hal - le - lu - jah! Hal-le-lu-jah! Hal-le-lu-jah!
God om-ni - - po-tent reign - eth. Hal-le-lu-jah! Hal-le-lu-jah! Hal-le-lu-jah!
God om-ni - - - po-tent reign - eth. Hal-le-lu-jah! Hal-le-lu-jah!
8

Hal-le-lu-jah! Hal-le-lu-jah! Hal-le-lu-jah! Hal-le-lu-jah! Hal - le - lu - jah! Hal -
for the Lord God om - ni - - po - tent reign - - eth. Halle-lu-jah!
for the Lord God om - ni - - po - tent reign - - eth. Hal-
Hal-le-lu-jah! Hal-le-lu-jah! Hal-le-lu-jah! Halle - lu - jah! Halle-lu-jah! Halle-
8 8 8

-le - lu - jah! The kingdom of this world is be - come the
Hal - le - lu - jah! The kingdom of this world is be - come the
- le - - lu - jah! The kingdom of this world is be - come the
- lu-jah! Halle-lu - jah! The kingdom of this world is be - come the

8vi. Ped. 8vi

king - dom of our Lord, and of his Christ, and of his Christ;
king - dom of our Lord, and of his Christ, and of his Christ;
king - dom of our Lord, and of his Christ, and of his Christ;
king - dom of our Lord, and of his Christ, and of his Christ; and he shall

and he shall reign for ev - er and ev - - -
reign for ev - er and ev - er, for ev - er and ev - er, and he shall

and
and he shall reign for ev - er and ev - - er, for ev - er
- er, and he shall reign for ev - er and ev - - - er,
reign, and he shall reign for ev - er, for ev - er, for ev - er, for
he shall reign for ev - er and ev - - er, King of kings,
and ev - er, for ev - er and ev - er, King of kings,
and he shall reign for ev - er and ev - er, for ev - er and
ev - er and ev - er, for ev - er, for ev - er and ev - er, for ev - er and
and Lord of lords,
and Lord of lords,
- ev - er, Hal-le - lu - jah! Hal-le - lu - jah! for ev - er and

King of kings, ...

for ev - er and

ev - er, Hal-le - lu - jah! Hal-le - lu - jah! for ev - er and

ev - er, Hal-le - lu - jah! Hal-le - lu - jah! and Lord of lords, ...

for ev - er and

ev - er, Hal-le - lu - jah! Hal-le - lu - jah! for ev - er and

ev - er, Hal-le - lu - jah! Hal-le - lu - jah! King of kings, ...

for ev - er and

ev - er, Hal-le - lu - jah! Hal-lo - lu - jah for ev - er and

and Lord of lords, and Lord of
ev - er, Hal-le - lu - jah! Hal-le - lu - jah! King of kings, and Lord of
ev - er, Hal-le - lu - jah! Hal-le - lu - jah! King of kings, and Lord of
ff
Ped.
lords, and he shall reign, and
lords, and he shall reign, and he shall
lords, and he shall reign for ev - er,
lords, and he shall reign for ev - er and ev - er,
he shall reign for ev - er and ev - er, for ev - er and
reign for ev - er and ev - er, King of kings, for ev - er and
and he shall reign for ev - er and ev - er, King of kings
and he shall reign for ev - er and ev - er, King of kings, for ev - er and

ev - er, Hal-le-lu-jah! Hal-le - lu-jah! and he shall
ev - er, and Lord of lords, Hal-le-lu-jah! Hal-le - lu-jah! and
.... and Lord of lords,.......................... and he shall
ev - er, and Lord of lords, Hal-le-lu-jah! Hal-le - lu-jah! and he shall
reign for ev - er, for ev - er and ev - - er, King of
be shall reign for ev - er and ev - - er, King of....
reign for ev - er, for ev - er and ev - - er, King of....
Ped.
kings! and Lord of lords! King of kings! and Lord of
kings! and Lord of.... lords! King of kings! and Lord of....
kings! and Lord of.... lords! King of kings! and Lord of....

lords, and he shall reign for ever and ev - -
lords, and he shall reign for ev - er and ev - - -
lords, and he shall reign for ev - er and ev - - -
lords, and he shall reign for ev - er and ev - er and ev - - -
- er, King of kings! and Lord of lords! Hal-le-lu-jah! Hal-le-
- er, for ev-er and ev-er, for ev-er and ev-er, Hal-le-lu-jah! Hal-le-
- er, for ev-er and ev-er, for ev-er and ev-er, Hal-le-lu-jah! Hal-le-
Ped. 8va.
- lu-jah! Hal-le-lu-jah! Hal-le-lu-jah! Hal - le - lu - jah!
- lu-jah! Hal-le-lu-jah! Hal-le-lu-jah! Hal - le - lu - jah!
- lu-jah! Hal-le-lu-jah! Hal-le-lu-jah! Hal - le - lu - jah!

No. 4. AND THE GLORY OF THE LORD

- - - ed, and the glo - ry, the glory of the Lord
shall be re - - veal - ed, be re - veal - -
glo - ry, the glory of the Lord shall be re - -
shall be re - veal - ed,
shall be re - veal'd, and the glo - ry, the glory of the Lord shall be
- - - - - - - - - - - - - - - - ed, and the glo - ry, the glory of the Lord shall be
- veal - - - - - - ed, and the glo - ry, the glory of the Lord shall be
re - veal - ed,
re - veal - ed, and all flesh shall
re - veal - ed,

see it to - geth - er,
and all flesh shall see it to - geth - er, For the
Pedals in 8va.
and all flesh shall see it to - geth - - - er ; For the mouth
and all flesh shall see it to - - geth - - er, and all
mouth of the Lord hath spok-en it ; and all
of the Lord hath spok - en it ;
flesh shall see it to - geth - - - er, and all flesh, and all flesh shall
flesh shall see it to - geth - - - er, and all flesh shall see it to-

and all - flesh shall see it to - geth - - er,
see it to - geth - er; and all flesh shall see it to - geth - - er;
- geth - - - er; the mouth of the Lord hath spo - ken it.
For the mouth of the Lord hath spo - ken it.
Pedals in 8va.
And the glo - ry, the glo-ry of the Lord,
And the glo - ry, the glo-ry of the Lord, and all
And the glo - ry, the glo-ry of the Lord, and all
and all flesh shall see it to - geth - er; the mouth of the
flesh shall see it to - geth - er; and the glo - ry, the
flesh shall see it, shall see it to - geth - er;
and all flesh shall see it to - geth - er;

Lord hath spok - en it;
glo-ry of the Lord shall be re - - veal - ed, and all
and all flesh
and all flesh
for the mouth of the Lord hath spok - - en
flesh shall see it to - geth - er; for the mouth
shall see it to - geth - er; the glo - ry, the glo-ry of the Lord shall
shall see it to - geth - er; and the
it, hath spok - - - - - - - - - en it.
of the Lord........................hath spok - en it; and all flesh
be re - veal - - - - - - - - - - - - - - - - ed, and all
glo - ry, the glo-ry of the Lord shall be re - veal - - ed,

and the glo - ry, the glo - ry, the glory of the
shall see it to - geth - er;
flesh shall see it to - geth - er;
and all flesh shall see it to - geth - er;
Lord shall be re - veal - - - - - ed,
and the glo - ry, the glory of the Lord shall be re - - veal - - -
and the glo - ry, the glory of the Lord
and the glo - ry, the glory of the Lord shall be re - -
8
and all flesh shall see it to-
- - ed, re - veal - ed, and all flesh shall see it to-
shall be re - - veal - - - - ed, and all flesh shall see it to-
- veal - - - - - - - ed, re - veal - - - - - ed; for the mouth of the

geth - er, to - geth - - er; For the mouth of the Lord.. ...
geth er, to - geth - - er; For the mouth of the Lord
geth - er, to - geth - - er; For the mouth of the Lord......
Lord hath spok - en it. For the mouth of the Lord
hath spok - en it, for the mouth of the
hath spok - en it, for the mouth of the
hath spok - en it, For the mouth of the Lord..... the
ADAGIO.
Lord.................... hath spok - - - - en it.
Lord.................... hath spok - - - - en it.
mouth of the Lord hath spok - - - - en it.
ADAGIO.
Pedals in 8va.

No. 6. CHORUS.—"SLEEPERS, WAKE! A VOICE IS CALLING."

CHORAL. *Con Moto.* ♩= 69. Matth. xxv. 1.

TREBLE. ALTO. TENOR. 8ve lower. BASS. ACCOMP.

Sleepers, wake! a voice is call - ing,..........................

Sleepers, wake! a voice is call - ing,..........................

Sleepers, wake! a voice is call - ing,..........................

It is the watchman on the walls;..........................

It is the watchman on the walls, the walls;..............

It is the watchman on the walls, the walls;..............

Thou Ci - ty of Je - ru - sa - lem!..................

Thou Ci - ty of Je - ru - sa - lem!..................

Thou Ci - ty of Je - ru - sa - lem!..................

For lo! the Bridegroom comes! A - rise, and take your lamps! Hal - le - lu -
For lo! the Bridegroom comes! A - rise, and take your lamps! Hal - le - lu -
For lo! the Bridegroom comes! A - rise, and take your lamps! Hal - le - lu -
mf
- jah! Awake! His kingdom is at hand!.................. Go
- jah! Awake! His kingdom is at hand!.................. Go
- jah! Awake! His kingdom is at hand!.................. Go
f
forth, go forth to meet your Lord!.......................................
forth, go forth to meet your Lord! go forth to meet your Lord!......
forth, go forth to meet your Lord! go....... ye forth to meet your Lord!
forth, go forth to meet your Lord! to meet your Lord!......
f

"He watching over Israel."

"ELIJAH"

Is - - ra - el, slumbers not, nor sleeps, slum - - bers not, nor sleeps.

Is - - - - ra - el, slum - - bers not, He slumbers not, nor sleeps.

- - bers not, nor sleeps, slum - - bers not, He slumbers not, nor sleeps, Shouldst thou,

not, nor sleeps, slum - - bers not, nor sleeps.

dim. *p* *dimin.* *cres.*

Shouldst thou, walking in grief,

Shouldst thou, walk - ing in grief, lan - - guish, He will quicken

walk - ing in grief, lan - guish, He will quicken thee; Shouldst thou, walking in grief, . . .

cres

lan - guish; He will quicken thee, He. . . . . will quick-en thee; Shouldst thou,

thee, ... will quick en thee, ... He will quick - - - - en thee;

. . . . in grief, ... languish; He will quick - en thee, ... Shouldst thou,

Shouldst thou, walk-ing in grief, lan - guish; He, He. . . . . will quicken

cres.

walk - ing in grief, lan - guish; He will, He...... will quicken thee;
Shouldst thou, walk- ing in grief, lan - - - guish, Shouldst thou, walking in grief,
walk - ing in grief,.................. in grief......... lan - guish; He will quick-en
thee; Shouldst thou, walking in grief, lan - guish; He will quicken
cres.
Shouldst thou, walking in grief, lan - guish, walk - ing in grief, lan - guish;
lan - guish, He will quicken thee; Shouldst thou, walking in grief languish;
thee, will quick - en thee; Shouldst thou, walk - ing in grief, lan - guish;
thee............ He will quicken thee; Shouldst thou, walk-ing in grief, lan - guish;
dim.
He will quicken thee, He........ will quicken thee, He, watching o - ver
He will quicken thee, He will quicken thee, He, watching
He will quicken thee, He will quicken thee, Shouldst thou, walking in grief,
He will quicken, He................ will quicken thee,
dim.
diminuendo.

Is - rael, slumbers not, nor sleeps, Shouldst thou, walk-ing in grief, lan - guish;
o - ver Is - ra - el, slumbers not, Shouldst thou, walk - - ing in grief, lan -
lan - guish; He will quick-en thee, He, watching o - ver Is - ra - el,
p
He, watching o - - ver Is - - ra - el, slum - - - bers
He will quick- en thee. He, watching o - ver Is - ra - el, slum - bers not, nor
f
dim.
- guish; He will quick-en thee...... He slum - bers not, slum - - bers not, nor
slum - bers not, nor sleeps ... He slum - bers not...... He slum - - bers
cres.
not, - nor sleeps.......... He slum - - bers not, nor
sleeps.... He slum - bers not, He slum - bers not, He watching
sleeps; He.......... slum - bers not, He slum - bers not; He watch - ing
not,...... He slum - bers not, He slum - bers not; He
sleeps; He slum - - bers not, He slum - bers not, He slum - bers
p

o - ver Is - ra - el, slum - bers not, nor sleeps; .... He slum -
Is - - ra - el, slum - bers not, nor sleeps; He........ slum
slum - - bers not,...... He slum - bers not,..... He slumbers
not, He slum - - bers not, nor sleeps; He slum - - bers
- bers not, He slum - bers not, sleeps not, He, watch - - ing Is -
- bers not, He slumbers not, sleeps not, He, watch-ing
not, He slum - bers not, sleeps not, He, watch -
not, He slum-bers not, sleeps not, He, watching
- - ra - el, slum - - - bers not, nor sleeps.
Is - ra - el, slum - - - bers not, nor sleeps.
- ing......... slum - - - bers not, nor sleeps.
Is - ra - el,........ slum - bers not, nor sleeps.

Gloria, Mozart's 12th Mass.

- a, De - o glo - ri - a, glo - ri - a in ex - cel - sis. De - - - - - - -
Lord glorious is thy name, glo - ri - ous is thy name, Al - migh - - - - - -
- - a, De - o, glo - ri - a, glo - ri - a in ex - cel - sis, De - o, in ex - -
Lord, glo-rious is thy name, glo - ri - ous is thy name, Al - migh-ty, glo - rious
- - a, De - o glo - ri - a, glo - ri - a, in ex - cel - sis, De - o, in ex - -
Lord, glo-rious is thy name, glo - ri - ous is thy name, Al-migh - ty, glo - rious
- - a, De - o glo - ri - a, glo - ri - a in ex - cel-sis, De - o
Lord, glo-rious is thy name, glo - ri-ous is thy name, Al - migh-ty,
- - cel-sis, De - - - o, in ex - cel - sis, De - - - o in ex - cel-sis, De - - -
is thy name, O Lord, glo-rious is thy name, O Lord, glo-rious is thy name, O
- cel-sis, De - - o in ex - cel-sis, De - - - o in ex - cel - sis, De - -
is thy name, O Lord, glo-rious is thy name, O Lord, glo-rious is thy name, O
in ex - cel-sis, De - - - o, De - - -
glo-rious, glorious is thy name, is thy

- o in ex - cel - sis, De - o glo - ri - a et in ter - ra
- ty, glorious is thy name, Al - migh - ty Lord; all the an-gels
- o in ex - cel - sis, De - o glo - ri - a et in ter - ra
Lord, glorious is thy name, Al - migh - ty Lord; all the an-gels
- o in ex - cel - sis, De - o glo - ri - a et in ter - ra
Lord, glorious is thy name, Al - migh - ty Lord; all the an-gels
- o in ex - cel - sis, De - o glo - ri - a et in ter - ra
name, glorious is thy name, Al - migh - ty Lord; all the an-gels
Without Trumpets
8 va
p
f
pax, pax, pax ho - mi - ni - bus et in ter - ra,
stand, stand round a - bout thy throne, all the an - gels
pax, pax, pax ho - mi - ni - bus et in ter - ra,
stand, stand round a - bout thy throne, all the an - gels
pax, pax, pax ho - mi - ni - bus et in ter - ra,
stand, stand round a - bout thy throne, all the an - gels
pax, pax, pax ho - mi - ni - bus et in ter - ra,
stand, stand round a - bout thy throne, all the an - gels
Choir.

pax, pax, pax ho - mi - ni - bus; bo - næ,
stand, stand round a - bout thy throne; Let all
pax, pax, pax ho - mi - ni - bus; bo-næ,
stand, stand round a - bout thy throne; Let all
pax, pax, pax ho - mi - ni - bus; bo-næ,
stand, stand round a - bout thy throne; Let all
pax, pax, pax ho - mi - ni - bus; bo-næ,
stand, stand round a - bout thy throne, Let all
Swell Hautboy.
bo - næ vo - lun - ta - tis, vo - lun - ta - tis,
na - tions bow be-fore thee, bow before thee
bo - næ vo - lun - ta - tis, vo-lun-ta - tis,
na - tions bow be-fore thee, bow be-fore thee,
bo - næ vo - lun - ta - tis, vo-lun - ta - tis, bo - næ
na - tions bow be-fore thee, bow before thee let all
bo - næ vo-lun - ta - - tis, vo-lun - ta - tis,
na - tions bow be-fore thee, bow be-fore thee,
Full Swell.

Cres. *f*
bo - næ, bo - næ vo - lun - ta - tis, bo - næ, bo - næ, bo - næ vo - lun - ta - - - -
let all na-tions bow be - fore.. Thee, let all, let all na-tions bow be - fore....

Cres. *f*
bo - næ, bo - næ vol - un - ta - - tis, bo - næ, bo - - næ, bo - næ vo - lun - ta - - - -
let all na-tions bow be - fore Thee, let all, let all na-tions bow be - fore.....

Cres. *f*
bo - næ, bo - næ, vo - lun - ta - tis, bo - næ, bo - - næ, bo - næ vo - lun - ta - - - -
let all na-tions bow be - fore Thee, let all, let all na-tions bow be - fore

Cres. *f*
bo - næ, bo - næ vo - lun - ta - tis, bo - næ, bo - næ, bo - næ vo - lun - ta - - - -
let all na-tions bow be - fore Thee, let all, let all na-tions bow be - fore

f >
Full
Cres. *f*

Cres. *f*
tis, bo - næ, bo - næ vo - lun - ta - tis, bo - næ, bo - næ,
Thee, let all na-tions bow be - fore Thee, let all, let all

f
- tis bo - næ, bo - næ vo - lun - ta - tis, bo - næ, bo - næ,
Thee, *mf* *let all na-tions bow be - fore Thee, let all, let all*

Cres. *f*
- tis, bo - - næ, bo - næ, bo - næ vo - lun - ta - tis, bo - næ, bo - - næ,
Thee, let all, let all nations bow be - fore Thee, let all, let all

Cres. *f*
- tis, bo - næ, bo - næ vo - lun - ta - tis, bo - næ, bo - næ,
Thee, let all na-tions bow be - fore Thee, let all, let all

Full Swell. *f* >
mp Choir. Cres. *f*

bo - næ vo - lun - ta - - tis,
na-tions bow be - fore Thee,
bo - næ vo - lun - ta - - tis,
and de-clare thy wond'rous works,
bo - næ vo - lun - ta - - tis,
na-tions bow be - fore Thee,
bo - næ vo - lun - ta - - tis,
and de-clare thy won'drous works,
bo - næ vo - lun - ta - - tis,
na-tions bow be - fore Thee,
bo - næ vo - lun - ta - - tis,
and de-clare thy wond'rous works,
bo - næ vo - lun - ta - - tis,
na-tions bow be - fore Thee,
bo - næ vo - lun - ta - - tis,
and de-clare thy wond'rous works,
Ped.
bo - næ vo - lun - ta - - tis.
and de-clare thy wond'rous works.
Lau - da - mus,
We praise thee,
p
bo - næ vo - lun - ta - - tis.
and de-clare thy wond'rous works.
Lau - da - mus,
We praise thee,
p
bo - næ vo - lun - ta - - tis.
and de-clare thy wond'rous works.
Lau - da - mus,
We praise thee,
p
bo - næ vo - lun - ta - - tis.
and de-clare thy wond'rous works.
Lau - da - mus,
We praise thee,
p
p

be - ne - di - ci - mus, a - do - ra - mus, glo - ri - fi - ca - mus.
we give thanks to thee, we a - dore thee, we glo - ri - fy thee.
Gra - ti - as a - gi - mus, ti - bi prop - ter mag-nam, glo - ri - am tu - am,
Lord, we a - dore thee, we bless thee; Lord, we thank thee for thy great glo - ry,

prop - ter mag - nam,
Lord we thank thee,
prop-ter mag-nam,
Lord we thank thee,
glo - ri-am tu-am,
for thy great glo-ry,
glo - ri-am tu-am,
for thy great glory,
prop - ter mag - nam, glo - ri - am; tu - am, glo - ri - am tu - am, glo - ri - am
Lord we thank thee for thy great glo - ry, for thy great glo - ry, for thy great

f

tu - - - am. Do - - mi - ne De - us,
glo - - - ry. Heav'n is thy throne, and

tu - - - am. Do - - mi - ne De - us,
glo - - - ry. Heav'n is thy throne, and

tu - - - am. Do - - mi - ne De - - us,
glo - - - ry. Heav'n is thy throne, and

tu - - - am. Do - - mi - ne De - us,
glo - - - ry. Heav'n is thy throne, and

Cres.

Full with Trum:pts.

8 vi.

Deus Rex Cœ - les - tis. De - - - us Pa - ter om - - ni - - - - - - po -
earth is thy foot - stool. Thou art King o - ver all the

Deus Rex Cœ - les - tis. De - - - us Pa - ter om - - ni - - - - - - po -
earth is thy foot - stool. Thou art King o - ver all the

Deus Rex Cœ - les - tis. De - - - us Pa - ter om - - ni - - - - - - po -
earth is thy foot - stool. Thou art King o - ver all the

Deus Rex Cœ - les - tis. De - - - us Pa - ter om - - ni - - - - - - po -
earth is thy foot - stool. Thou art King o - ver all the

- tens. Do-mi-ne Fi - - - li u - ni-ge-ni-
world. Glo-ri-ous is thy name, is thy name, O

- tens. Do-mi-ne Fi - - - li u - ni-ge-ni-
world. Glo-ri-ous is thy name, is thy name, O

- tens. Do-mi-ne Fi - - - li u - ni-ge-ni-
world. Glo-ri-ous is thy name, is thy name, O

- tens. Do-mi-ne Fi - - - li u - ni-ge-ni-
world. Glo-ri-ous is thy name, is thy name, O

Ped.

- te, Je - su Chris - - te, Do-mi-ne De-us, Agnus De - i, Fi - li - us Pa-tris,
Lord, glo-rious is thy name. Blessing and hon-or be to God, for ev - er and ev - er,

- te, Je - su Chris - - te, Do-mi-ne De-us, Agnus De - i, Fi - li - us Pa-tris,
Lord, glo-rious is thy name. Blessing and hon-or be to God, for ev - er and ev - er,

- te, Je - su Chris - - te, Do-mi-ne De-us, Agnus De - i, Fi - li - us Pa-tris,
Lord, glo-rious is thy name. Blessing and hon-or be to God, for ev - er and ev - er,

- te, Je - su Chris - - te,
Lord, glo-rious is thy name.

Fi-li-us Pa - - - tris, Fi-li-us Pa - - - tris.
for ev-er ev - er - - more, forev-er ev - er - more.
Fi-li-us Pa - - - tris, Fi-li-us Pa - - - tris.
for-ev-er ev - er - - more, forev-er ev - er - more.
Fi-li-us Pa - - - tris, Fi-li-us Pa - - - tris.
for-ev-er ev - er - - more, forev-er ev - er - more.
Fi-li-us Pa - - - tris, Fi-li-us Pa - - - tris,
for-ev-er ev - er - - more, forev-er ev - er - more
Full without Trumpet.
Do - mine De - us, Ag-nus De - i, Fi-li-us Pa - - tris. Do - mi-ne De - us,
Blessing and hon-or be to God, for ev-er and ev - er - more. Blessing and honor
Do - mine De - us, Ag-nus De - i, Fi-li-us Pa - - tris. Do - mi-ne De - us,
Blessing and hon-or be to God, for ev-er and ev - er - more. Blessing and honor
Do - mine De us, Ag-nus De - i, Fi-li-us Pa - - tris. Do - mi-ne De - us,
Blessing and hon-or be to God, for ev-er and ev - er - more. Blessing and honor
Do - mine De - us, Ag-nus De - i, Fi-li-us Pa - - tris. Do - mi-ne De - us,
Blessing and hon-or be to God, for ev-er and ev - er - more. Blessing and honor

Ag-nus De-i, Fi-li-us Pa - tris, Fi-li-us, Fi-li-us Pa - tris.
be to God, for ev-er and ev-ermore, blessing for-ev-er and ev - er-more.
Ag-nus De-i, Fi-li-us Pa - tris. Fi-li-us, Fi-li-us Pa - tris.
be to God, for ev-er and ev-ermore, blessing for ev-er and ev - er-more.
Ag-nus De-i, Fi-li-us Pa - tris, Fi-li-us, Fi-li-us Pa - tris.
be to God, for ev-er and ev-ermore, blessing for ev er and ev - er-more.
Ag-nus De-i, Fi-li-us Pa - tris, Fi-li-us, Fi-li-us Pa - tris.
be to God, for ev-er and ev-ermore, blessing for ev-er and ev - er-more.
8 va.

THE HARP THAT ONCE THROUGH TARA'S HALLS.

Written by THOMAS MOORE.

Observe the crescendo and diminuendo marks strictly in singing 1st verse.

sleeps the pride of form - er days, So glo - ry's thrill is
free - dom now so sel - dom wakes, The on - ly throb she
hearts that once beat high for praise, Now feel that pulse nc
pp
when some heart in - dig - nant breaks, To show that still sh

THE STAR SPANGLED BANNER.

TO BE SUNG AS FOLLOWS;

1st Verse, Basses in Unison, 1st 16 Measures only. Tenors in Unison, 2d 16 Measures. 2d Verse, Sopranos and Altos in Duet. 3d Verse, Tenors and Basses in Duet.

Originally written by Francis S. Keys, with an additional verse by W. T. W. Ball.

ramparts we watched were so gal - lant - ly streaming, And the rocket's red
glo - ry to dim which now is un - clouded: Not as North or as
pow'r that has made and preserved us a na - tion. Then con - quer we
glare, the bombs bursting in air, Gave proof thro' the night that our
South in the fu - ture we'll stand, But as bro - thers u - nit - ed throng
must, when our cause it is just, And this be our mot - to*—"In
Flag was still there; O say, does that star - spangled ban - ner yet
out our broad land, And the star - spangled ban - ner for - ev - er shall
God is our trust," And the star - spangled ban - ner in tri - umph shall
wave, O'er the land of the free and the home of the brave.
8

CHORUS.
SOPRANO.
1. O say, does that star - spangled ban ner - yet wave, O'er the land of the
ALTO.
2. And the star spangled ban - ner for - ev - er shall wave, O'er the land of the
TENOR.
3. And the star-spangled ban - ner for - ev - er shall wave, O'er the land of the
BASS.
PIANO.
free and the home of the brave.
free and the home of the brave.
free and the home of the brave.
No Symphony after 3d verse.
8

LUTHER'S JUDGMENT HYMN.

Eight Bars will first be played by the Orchestra or Organ as an Introduction.

CHORUS.
SOPRANO.
Great God, what do I see and hear! The end of things crea - a - -
ALTO.
Great God, what do I see and hear! The end of things cre - a - -
TENOR.
Great God, what do I see and hear! The end of things cre - a - -
BASS.
Great God, what do I see and hear! The end of things cre - a - -
ACCOMP.
TRUMPET SWELL.
Ad lib.
FULL ORGAN.
8ves.
ted. The Judge of mankind does ap - pear On clouds of glo - ry
ted. The Judge of mankind does ap - pear On clouds of glo - ry
ted. The Judge of mankind does ap - pear On clouds of glo - ry
ted. The Judge of mankind does ap - pear On clouds of glo - ry
TRUMPET.
Ad lib.
TRUMPET.
Ad lib.

seat - ed.
The trumpet sounds, the graves re - store
The dead which
seat - ed.
The trumpet sounds, the graves re - store
The dead which
seat - ed.
The trumpet sounds, the graves re - store
The dead which
seat - ed.
The trumpet sounds, the graves re - store
The dead which
TRUMPET.
TRUMPET.
they contained be - fore.
Pre-pare, my soul, to meet Him.
they contained be - fore.
Pre-pare, my soul, to meet Him.
they contained be - fore.
Pre-pare, my soul, to meet Him.
they contained be - fore.
Pre-pare, my soul, to meet Him.
TRUMPET.
TRUMPET.
dim.

A HYMN OF PEACE.

Written for the National Peace Festival, by Dr. O. W. Holmes.

TO THE MUSIC OF

KELLER'S AMERICAN HYMN.

ff
Fly to our ark like the storm-beat - en dove! Fly to our ark on the
Breeze of the prai - rie and breath of the sea, Meadow and mountain and
ff
Bid the full breath of the or - gan re - ply, Let the loud tem - pest of
ff
mf cresc: f
wings of the dove,— Speed o'er the far - sounding bil - lows of song,
for - est and sea! Sweet is the fragrance of myr - tle and pine,
mf cresc: f
voi - ces re - ply,— Roll its long surge like the earth - shaking main!
mf cresc: f
mf cresc: f

Crowned with thine o - live - leaf gar - land of love,— An - gel of
Sweet - er the in - cense we of - fer to thee, Broth - ers once
Swell the vast song till it mounts to the sky!— An - gels of
Peace, thou hast wait - ed too long!
more round this al - tar of thine!
Beth - le - hem, ech - o the strain!

OVERTURE TRIUMPHALE.

A symphonic work for a full Orchestra, on the American National Air of "HAIL COLUMBIA," Closing with a Chorus for mixed voices, with Orchestral, Organ and other Accompaniments. Composed for the National Peace Jubilee, by C. C. CONVERSE.

CHORUS PART.

Sopranos who cannot sing A & B as they occur in the following arrangement of Hail Columbia, should sing the small notes.

pp
ANDANTE.
CLARIONET.
368
ALLEGRO.
Cres.
f
Piu: f
ff
VIOLIN.
TIMPANI.

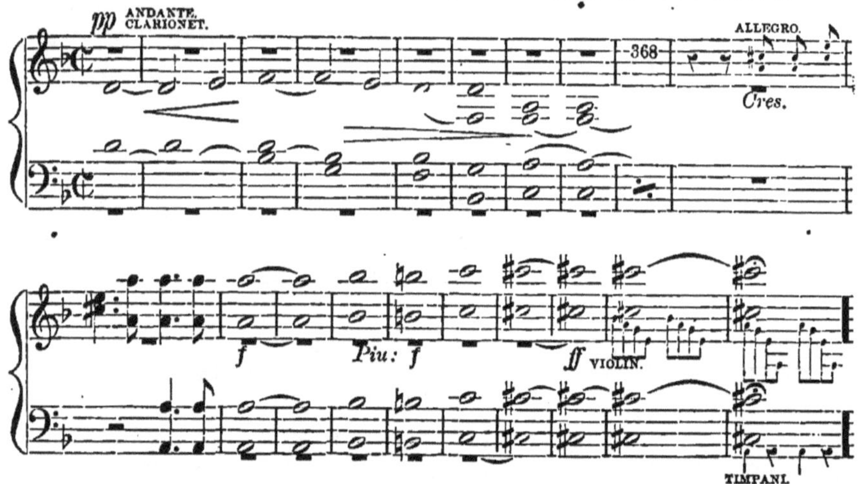

HAIL COLUMBIA.

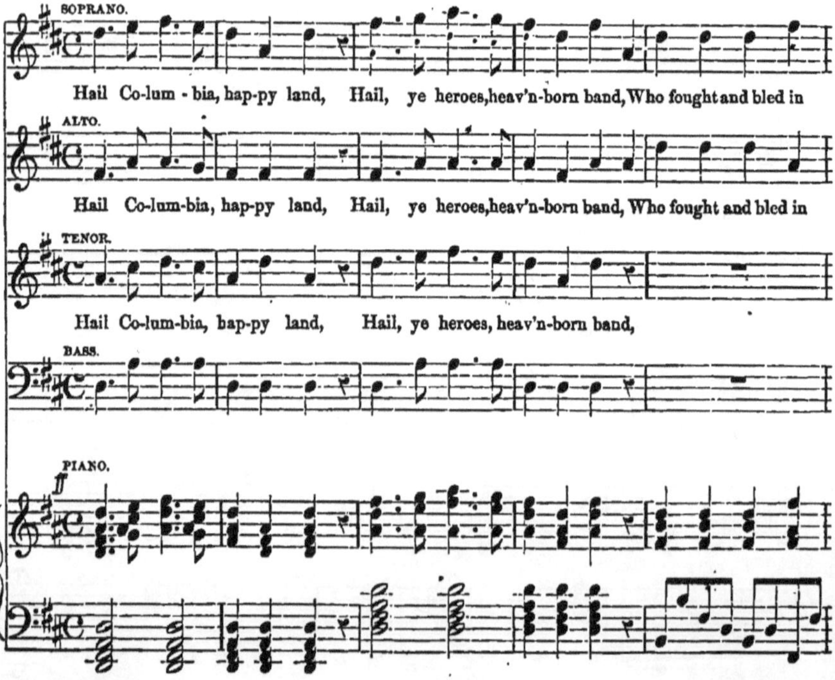

SOPRANO.
Hail Co-lum - bia, hap-py land, Hail, ye heroes, heav'n-born band, Who fought and bled in
ALTO.
Hail Co-lum-bia, hap-py land, Hail, ye heroes, heav'n-born band, Who fought and bled in
TENOR.
Hail Co-lum-bia, hap-py land, Hail, ye heroes, heav'n-born band,
BASS.
PIANO.
ff

Freedom's cause, who fought and bled in Freedom's cause, And when the storm of war was done, En -
Freedom's cause,
Freedom's cause, And when the storm of war was done, En -
Who fought and bled in Freedom's cause, And when the storm of war was done, En -
joyed the peace your valor won.
Let Independence
joyed the peace your valor won.
Let Independence
joyed the peace your valor won.
Let Independence
ff

be your boast,
Ev - er mind - ful
be · your boast,
Ev - er mind - ful
be your boast,
Ev - er mind - ful
what it cost.
Firm, u - ni - ted let us be,
what it cost.
Firm, u - ni - ted let us be,
what it cost.
Firm, u - ni - ted let us be,

Rally - ing round our lib - er - ty! As a band of brothers joined,
Rally - ing round our lib - er - ty! As a band of brothers joined,
Rally - ing round our lib - er - ty! As a band of brothers joined,
Peace and safe - ty we shall find.
Peace and safe - ty we shall find.
Peace and safe - ty we shall find.

Octaves.
mf
Peace shall find.
Peace shall find.
Peace shall find.
8va.
LOCO.
VIOLINS.

Peace shall find.
Peace shall find.
Peace shall find.
ff
ff
Peace, Peace we shall find....................
Peace, Peace we shall find....................
Peace, Peace we shall find....................

GOD KEEP OUR COUNTRY FREE EVERMORE.

Written by Rev. S. F. SMITH, D. D.

AMERICA.

Andante.
Written by Rev. S. F. SMITH, D. D.
SOPRANO.
1. My coun - try, 'tis of thee, Sweet land of lib - er - ty,
ALTO.
2. My na - tive coun - try, thee—Land of the no - ble, free—
3. Let mu - sic swell the breeze, And ring from all the trees,
TENOR. 1st & 2d.
4. Our fa - thers' God, to thee, Au - thor of lib - er - ty,
BASS.
Of thee I sing; Land where my fa - thers died, Land of the
Thy name—I love; I love thy rocks and rills, Thy woods and
Sweet freedom's song; Let mor - tal tongues a - wake; Let all that
To thee we sing: Long may our land be bright With freedom's
pil - grim's pride, From eve - ry mountain's side Let free - dom ring.
tem - pled hills; My heart with rap - ture thrills Like that a - bove.
breathe par - take; Let rocks their si - lence break, The sound pro - long.
ho - ly light; Pro - tect us by thy might, Great God our King.

CHORUS. "Night's Shade no longer."

Quartett
Beaming with bright - ness, morning ad - van - ces, Smiling with pleas - ure,
Beaming with bright - ness, morning ad - van - ces, Smiling with pleas - ure,
p
welcomes the day.
Chorus.
p
Beaming with bright - ness, morning ad - van - ces,
welcomes the day.
Beaming with bright - ness, morning ad - van - ces,
f
p
1st time.
2d time
Smiling with pleas - ure, welcomes the day. day. Beam - ing with bright - ness,
Smiling with pleas - ure, welcomes the day. day. Beam - ing with bright - ness,
1st.
2d.
p
tr tr tr

morn - ing ad - van - - ces, Smil - ing with pleasure, wel - comes the day,
morn - ing ad - van - - ces, Smil - ing with pleasure, wel - comes the day,
welcomes the day,...... welcomes the day,.... Smiling with pleas - ure,
welcomes the day,...... welcomes the day,...... Smiling with pleas - ure,
welcomes the day, the day, the day, the day.......
welcomes the day, the day, the day, the day.....

ANVIL CHORUS, FROM "IL TROVATORE."

f Chorus in Unison.
Proud - ly our ban - - - ner now gleams with gold - en lus - tre!
f
Bright - er each star shines in the glo - rious clus - ter!
Lib - er - - ty for - ev - er - more! And Peace, and U - nion, And Peace, and
1o. D.C. 2do.
U - nion throughout our hap - py land. land.
ff
D.C.

www.ingramcontent.com/pod-product-compliance
Lightning Source LLC
Chambersburg PA
CBHW031440280326
41927CB00038B/1400

* 9 7 8 3 3 3 7 2 2 2 1 9 2 *